The Circle – Adult Guide

The goal of *The Circle* is to give a sense of hope and inspiration to children who struggle with their sense of significance and place in this world. This story is about a character's desire to feel as though he belongs and the journey that ensues, leading him to a place of self-love and self-acceptance. With some guidance and help from an emotionally skilled adult, this book can be utilized as a therapeutic or reparative experience for the child.

While this story is overall inspirational and validating in nature, it may bring up some negative feelings for some children, which is completely normal and positive to produce change. This story can offer children the opportunity to explore, express and find solutions to these problems. The intent for this book is to encourage children to explore an issue that they may not otherwise want or have the opportunity to discuss. In this case the goals are to 1) validate that other children and human beings have these challenging experiences, 2) relieve the child's stress surrounding these types of events by talking and listening to the child's feelings and concerns in a compassionate manner, and 3) reinforce ways to constructively address these issues in real life.

It is a standard thought in psychology that often what a person believes is more important than what he knows. In other words, it is an individual's perspective that matters more than the reality of the situation. A child's perspective is formed by the world in which he lives every day. A child's self-value is based on his experiences with the world and the messages that he accepts as reality. It is our obligation as responsible adults to pay attention to the child's world in order to have an acute awareness of the repetitive messages he is given and how that child perceives these messages. Then, we must help guide the child in promoting a healthy identity based on a secured reality.

No matter who is utilizing this book, whether you are a parent, teacher, clinician or other caregiver, it is recommended the topics presented be discussed with the child as he or she is reading or listening to the story. Each child has a unique history with varying emotional circumstances and levels of emotional regulation. Please seek help from a qualified professional or expert if you need assistance with your particular situation.

The Circle

A Story about Accepting and Being Yourself

Written by Brady Gunther and Jessica Beasley Gunther, LCSW
Art by Jennifer Matthews Nickel

ISBN-13:978-0692425985 SoulWell Press
ISBN-10: 0692425985

"Dedicated to all those who feel they don't belong."
Brady Gunther, age 10

"A special dedication to my children who bravely face this world with resilience and compassion. I am continually amazed by their courage to express themselves and be the truly genuine human beings whom their father and I adore."

Jessica Beasley Gunther, LCSW & MOM

It was a regular, sunny day in the perfectly geometric village of Shapetowne. The sky was blue, the air was fresh, and all sorts of young shapes were playing soccer in the park or swinging in perfect arcs on the playground. It seemed as if everyone was having fun and talking together happily, except for one lonely and sad shape. Mr. Circle didn't feel perfect OR happy. He thought that maybe he was the only shape to ever feel that way.

None of the other shapes seemed to pay much attention to him and he sometimes had trouble asking them to play. He had tried to play with the other kids, but they often said no or would tease him. Sometimes they would trip him while he played soccer, make fun of him for being too round or pick him last to be on the softball team. Mr. Circle felt insulted and sad when this happened, so he'd lost the courage to even ask. He felt like nobody in Shapetowne liked or appreciated him.

While Mr. Circle was strolling by the park, a soccer ball flew by his head. As Mr. Square chased the ball over to where Mr. Circle was standing he thought to himself, *oh no, here we go again.* Mr. Square had a habit of making fun of Mr. Circle. But before Mr. Circle could walk away, Mr. Square stopped and looked squarely at him saying, "You are dumb because you have no sides." Feeling ashamed and embarrassed, Mr. Circle quickly walked away.

When he looked around the village he saw many other shapes talking, playing and having fun without a care. He kept thinking about what Mr. Square had said and noticed that none of the other shapes were round. He really did stand out because he was so different from the others. *Maybe, Mr. Square was right,* he thought. *Maybe I am dumb because I have no sides.*

Mr. Circle decided right then that he was going to have to find a way to fit in with these other shapes. He decided to pay a visit to Magic Chicken, Shapetowne's most powerful magician. Legend has it that Magic Chicken came to be after a dark and stormy day in Shapetowne many years ago. It is said that a lightning bolt struck a chicken coop when a tornado hit the outskirts of the village. Since that day, mysterious Magic Chicken has helped save many villagers from accidents, illnesses and other catastrophes. *If Magic Chicken could help all of those other shapes, surely he could help me with my problem,* thought Mr. Circle.

Mr. Circle was desperate to figure out a solution to his problem, so he bravely approached Magic Chicken and asked to be transformed into a square. The Magic Chicken didn't understand why Mr. Circle would want such a thing, but since he was in the business of helping shapes, he honored the request. Mr. Circle felt his curves straighten and right angles pop out at his newly formed corners. He rushed off, excited to show Mr. Square his new sides.

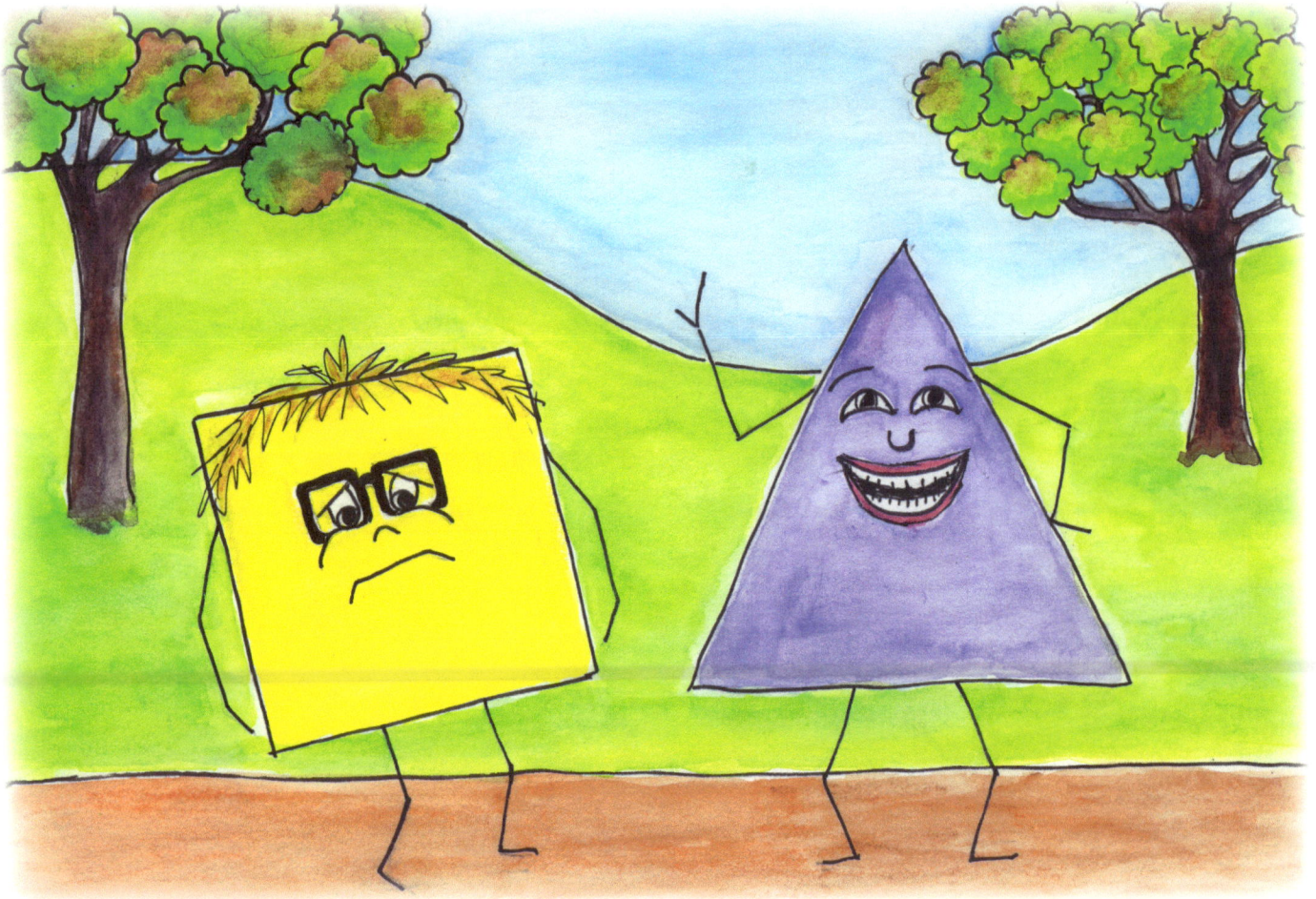

On the way to find Mr. Square, Mr. Circle ran into Mr. Triangle. "You know Mr. Circle... triangles are all the rage now, man!" Mr. Circle's heart sank as he listened to Mr. Triangle. He was beginning to think he made the wrong choice getting four new sides like Mr. Square.

It occurred to Mr. Circle that maybe to be accepted and liked he needed to be more like a triangle, so he went back to powerful Magic Chicken. Magic Chicken flapped his magical wings, and with a bright flash of light he again granted Mr. Circle his wish. With a curious popping sound, like a cork from a bottle, one of Mr. Circle's sides disappeared and the rest of them came together to form a triangle.

Feeling slightly odd, but hopeful in his new acute angles, Mr. Circle (the triangle) ran into Miss Cube. She looked him up and down and arrogantly sniffed, "Do you realize I have three dimensions and you only have two? Only the most AWESOME shapes are 3-D!" Mr. Circle's heart sank as he listened to Miss Cube talk about the virtues of being three-dimensional. He had to admit that it did sound pretty awesome to be 3-D. Suddenly, his acute angles didn't feel so cool.

He even ran into Miss Pentagon and Miss Cylinder, who also had opinions about how he should look and act. As they debated and argued with each other, Mr. Circle felt a tight aching pain in his stomach and his hands started to tingle. He was even more discouraged and overwhelmed.

He had thought all of the other shapes would be excited to see him with his new angles and kindly welcome him to play at the park. Though his angles felt very sharp and pointy, he thought it would be worth it if the other shapes would like him. Mr. Circle concluded that his uncomfortable new configuration didn't make a difference to any of them.

15

Disappointed that his plans had failed, Mr. Circle's eyes filled with tears as he came upon the wise Mr. Diamond. Mr. Diamond was a little bit different than the other shapes. He seemed kind as he stopped reading his book and looked at Mr. Circle. He softly asked Mr. Circle what was wrong. Mr. Circle told him of his day. He told him about wanting to play with the other shapes and not being included. "Why do they think I'm so ugly? Why don't they like me?" asked Mr. Circle.

"I don't think it is you they don't like. There are lots of reasons why some shapes are rude to other shapes. Sometimes shapes that bully aren't very happy on the inside, even if they look happy on the outside. They think that hurting others will make them feel better, but it usually doesn't work out that way. It only makes everyone feel bad. Maybe some of the shapes who seem rude are just confused by your changing appearance or haven't taken the time to get to know the real you. It's never okay for shapes to treat you so poorly. It's important to tell them how you feel when they say these things, so they will know they are hurting your feelings," replied Mr. Diamond.

16

He shone with brilliance as he explained that he believed Mr. Circle was a wonderful circle all along and it shouldn't matter what the other shapes thought. "If you try to change who you are to make others happy, nobody will be happy. Especially you." Mr. Diamond put his arm around Mr. Circle and reassured him that he wasn't alone in experiencing these feelings. "You have to learn about what makes you special. Once you've accepted yourself, you won't feel the need to change for others."

Mr. Circle raised his head and listened curiously as Mr. Diamond continued. He pointed out that Mr. Circle didn't seem like he was as compassionate as usual while wearing sharp edges. He also wasn't as creative when he was a square because he couldn't think outside of the box.

Mr. Circle wiped his eyes and nodded his head in agreement. He'd lost many of the best parts of who he was by trying to be someone different. Mr. Circle liked his circular parts and infinite shape. He liked that his sides didn't limit his creativity or curiosity. He liked being creative, determined, and compassionate. His face brightened as he realized he really liked all these parts of himself.

Eager to return to his familiar form, Mr. Circle decided to make one last visit to Magic Chicken. He asked his new friend, Mr. Diamond, if he would like to go with him. They set off together and found Magic Chicken magically clucking about near his coop. Mr. Circle made his final request of Magic Chicken.

"Magic Chicken, thank you so much for helping me out. Could I ask one final favor? May I please just be myself again?"

Magic Chicken was happy to see that Mr. Circle wanted to return to himself. With a wave of a magic chicken wing and a bright flash of light, Mr. Circle instantly curved back into a circle. He sighed with relief and happiness, glad that he didn't need to pretend to be any shape but his own.

Tips for Kids – by Brady, age 10

- Stand up for yourself against bullies. Get courageous by gaining higher self-esteem by liking things about yourself.

- Repeat in your head that you are a good person. Make a list of good things about yourself. If you need help coming up with a list you should ask someone you trust about what it is you flourish at and what they think about your strengths.

- Don't let rude people change who you are. Their rude comments aren't even always true. Tell yourself to just keep going and you'll get there one day!

- Don't give in to others trying to control you. Take away their power. Don't let them control you by making you upset. Have power over yourself and your own emotions.

- Be around people you like and who are kind to you. They shouldn't insult you. They should treat you with respect and as an equal.

- Get an adult because they can help you when you don't know what to do. Keep going to different adults until someone does help you.

- Sometimes you have to ignore the bullies. It's hard to do because you may want to lash out against them, but once you ignore them the first time, it becomes easier. It's like practicing skiing; you get better at it the more you practice. Tune out their insults. Walk away and find something positive to do.

- Don't let others bring you down. Remember the world doesn't revolve around them and their insults. You don't have to listen to insults. YOU matter. Their insults don't!

- Be yourself. Don't be what others want you to be. It doesn't matter how others do things. You don't have to fit in with the crowd. Being different and standing out is a good thing because it's helpful to the world that we each have unique qualities and strengths. Learn what your strengths are.

- If people bring you down and you are feeling upset, there are things you can do to feel better. Try to find people that appreciate you and who are kind. Try to talk to an adult you trust. Do things that make you happy, like playing with your favorite toy, journaling, drawing or reading. Remind yourself that you matter!

About the Author

Brady Gunther is a determined, intelligent, curious, creative and compassionate boy. He enjoys many activities such as computer games and creating his own worlds with words, sketching, Legos and Mindcraft. He believes strongly in social justice and is intrigued by history. He is also a budding musician, playing the guitar and drums. However, one of Brady's greatest loves is literature. He is mesmerized by a good story and loves being drawn into different worlds. He also enjoys sharing his own experiences and knowledge with others in hopes of making a difference in this world.

Jessica Gunther, LCSW is the currently the Clinical Director and Founder of SoulWell, a company dedicating to promoting mental health and wellness services. She has many years of experience working with individuals, families and organizations with an array of mental, emotional, psychosocial and educational challenges. While children and family welfare have been an important aspect of her career, her self-proclaimed greatest accomplishment has been raising her 3 young children. Her hope is to provide them with opportunities to view the world through a lens that encourages wellness, resilience, courage, compassion and authenticity.

Acknowledgements

Special thanks to the illustrator of *The Circle*, Jennifer Matthews Nickel. Thank you for donating your valuable time and talent to help bring this story to life through amazing illustrations. Your ability to work with Brady's vision was remarkable. For more information or to contact the illustrator please email admin@soulwell.me. Much appreciation also goes to Melissa Gunther for donating countless hours as the editor-in-chief of this project. Your attention to detail was significantly beneficial to the production of this book.. Also, thank you to our family and friends for being supportive of us during challenging times and celebratiing with us during the special moments.

A special thank you message from Brady

"I'd like to thank my mom, my Aunt Melissa and Jennifer Nickel for helping complete this book. I'd also like to thank my mom for always helping me through tough situations because without that this book wouldn't be possible." -- Brady

For more information about *The Circle*
and other therapeutic children's books, please go to
www.soulwell.me

www.ingramcontent.com/pod-product-compliance
Lightning Source LLC
Chambersburg PA
CBHW060842270326
41933CB00002B/173